REVOLUTIONARY PORTRAITS ■ REMBRANDT

This book is dedicated to:
My wife, Jill, who shares my love of
Rembrandt;
my grandchildren, Lauren and Bridie, who
have brought us so much joy; and
my old artist friend, Maurice Sumray,
rediscovered after so many years, who gave
me my first book on Rembrandt.

John Molyneux

Cover Self Portrait with Beret and
Turned-Up Collar (c1659). National
Gallery of Scotland, Edinburgh.
Left Self Portrait (1669).
Mauritshuis, The Hague.

Unless stated all illustrations are by
Rembrandt.

Rembrandt and revolution *John Molyneux*

First published in 2001 by

REDWORDS

1 Bloomsbury Street, London WC1B 3QE

www.redwords.org.uk

ISBN: 1 872208 15 0

Design and production by Roger Huddle

Printed by Interprint Ltd, Malta

4

Rembrandt
and revolution

John Molyneux

Publisher's note

This book is one of the first in a major series of **Revolutionary Portraits** from Redwords. The unifying theme in this eclectic collection is Marxism. Each author reviews the artist and their art in historical context. The focus is on the relationship between individual artists and larger historical forces, how each influences and shapes the other. All of the books in this series aim to lead us back to these works of art and music with new eyes and ears and a deeper understanding of how art can raise the human spirit.

Others books in the current series are Diego Rivera, Mozart and John Coltrane.

Redwords is a publishing collective specialising in art, history and literature from a socialist perspective.
We are linked to Bookmarks.

The Man with the Golden Helmet (c1648-50).
Staatliche Museen Preussischer Kulturbesitz,
Gemäldegalerie, Berlin.

The Jewish Bride (c1665). Rijksmuseum, Amsterdam.

Preface

Anyone writing about visual art has to come to terms with a basic problem—the inadequacy of writing in the face of the art. Just as the meaning of a poem, if the poem is any good, cannot be rendered in prose, so the 'meaning' of a good painting cannot be fully conveyed in words—otherwise what is the point of poetry or painting?

This general problem is particularly acute where Rembrandt is concerned because of his peculiar 'eloquence'. His work 'speaks' to us—emotionally, psychologically—with a directness unmatched even by masters such as Holbein and Titian. If you want to know how Rembrandt felt about his wife, Saskia, or his lover, Hendrickje Stoffels, or his religion, or beggars, looking at the paintings, etchings and drawings will tell you more than any words, including the words in this booklet.

So what is the justification for writing about art? What functions does it perform? In my opinion writing about art has three main useful functions. The first is that of a signpost—it is akin to the humble but vital guidebook or museum plan. It says, 'This way lies an important visual experience. Out of all the visual images with which you are bombarded, this is something worth really looking at.' The second is like that of a viewing platform from which to survey a natural or urban panorama—it provides a context or vantage point favourable to seeing the artwork clearly. It does this primarily by supplying information (technical, biographical and, especially, socio-historical) relevant to the work's production and reception. For example, Géricault's *Raft of the Medusa* is a mighty painting in itself, but it is easier to 'see' it properly, to grasp its power, if one is provided with the information that it was painted in response to an actual shipwreck which was controversial in the way that the recent Paddington rail crash and the sinking of the *Herald of Free Enterprise* at Zeebrugge were controversial. The third is as part of a wider argument about culture, society and history, as when Marx observed that 'Rembrandt painted the

Mother of God as a Dutch peasant woman' in order to make a point about ideology and material conditions in a debate about freedom of the press.

In this booklet I am concerned with all three of these functions, but especially with the second. Regarding the first, Rembrandt is hardly in need of my recommendation, but every little helps. Regarding the third, I hope that effective treatment of Rembrandt will serve as a demonstration of and recommendation for the method which I have endeavoured to use, namely historical materialism. But mainly my hope is that the wonder and depth of Rembrandt's art will appear all the more clearly when it is seen in its true historical context.

Titian, *Portrait of a Man* (c1512). National Gallery, London.

Portrait of Jacob Trip (c1661). National Gallery, London.

Diego Velázquez, *The Rokeby Venus* (c1644-48). National Gallery, London.

Portrait of Margaretha de Geer (1661). National Gallery, London.

Rembrandt and revolution

The subject of this study is the revolutionary art of Rembrandt van Rijn. Rembrandt's art, I shall argue, is revolutionary in three senses. First, Rembrandt was a revolutionary artist who pioneered a new way of painting (and of seeing) which overturned previous norms and conceptions of this art. Second, his art—a product of an actual social and political revolution in Holland during the second half of the 16th century—gave strong expression to many of the themes of that revolution. In this respect Rembrandt could be said to parallel David's relationship to the French Revolution. Third, his art was a product of a radical critical attitude to the outcome of a revolution that was probably the world's first properly constituted capitalist society. In this I think Rembrandt stands alone.

We should begin with the paintings.

The revolutionary character of Rembrandt's art

Rembrandt is thought of above all as a portrait painter, and portraiture is one of the three or four most important genres in the history of European painting. What kind of portraits were painted before Rembrandt? To answer this question look at one of Holbein's great portraits of *Henry VIII* (1539) or his even greater dual portrait of *The Ambassadors* (1533), or look at Giovanni Bellini's magnificent portrait of the *Doge Loredan of Venice*, or Titian's extraordinary *Portrait of a Man* (1512) (see page 12), which is possibly a self-portrait and certainly the most magnificent portrait of a sleeve in the history of the world. What kind of portraits were painted by the greatest of Rembrandt's contemporaries? Look at Van Dyck's huge equestrian portrait of Charles I (1638), or any of Velázquez's paintings of Philip IV of Spain or, one of his greatest masterpieces, so admired by Francis Bacon, the portrait of *Pope Innocent X* (1650).

These paintings are not chosen at random or for their typicality. They are put forward because, in my opinion, they represent the very best in the way of portraiture that European art had to offer in the 16th or early 17th century. Technically they are literally of the highest quality imaginable. Is it possible to conceive of painting that would achieve a higher degree of verisimilitude in the rendering of fur, silk or velvet than is found in these masterpieces? Is there in the whole of European art any work with greater command of precise significant detail than *The Ambassadors*? Was the dignity and sagacity of a ruler ever more convincingly depicted than in Bellini's *Doge Lovedan of Venice*? Have the shrewdness and cunning of power ever been more subtly revealed than in Velázquez's *Pope Innocent X*?

Yet set any or all of these great works alongside a major portrait by Rembrandt—for example that of *Jacob Trip* or that of his wife, *Margaretha de Geer* (both c1660), (see page 12), both of which hang in the National Gallery—and it is immediately apparent that with Rembrandt we are entering a different world. One key characteristic common to all the aforementioned pre-Rembrandt portraits is the concern to emphasise— through expression, pose and, above all, attire—the social status and position of the sitter. This is the func-tion of the supreme elegance of the Doge's hat, of the sensuous tangibility of Titian's sleeve, of the perfection of the sheen on Innocent X's red cape. In the Rembrandt portraits there is none of this. The clothes of both Jacob Trip and Margaretha de Geer are painted in such light and sketchy fashion that they simply merge into the dark background of the chiaroscuro without conveying any sense of grandeur or luxury, and the viewer's attention is focused overwhelmingly on the subjects' faces (and sec-ondarily on their hands). Moreover in both works there are specific formal devices to reinforce this effect. In the de Geer portrait it is the delicately but unobtrusively painted white ruff and cuffs which make her face and

1 The other artist of the time most renowned for his use of chiaroscuro is the Italian Caravaggio (1573-1610). However, in Caravaggio the technique is used not for psychological depth but in order to freeze and capture the dramatic moment. See for example *The Supper at Emmaus* (c1596-1602) in the National Gallery, where the 'moment' captured is the instant of the disciples' recognition of Christ.

hands stand out, and in the case of Jacob Trip it is the combination of the plain headband and scarf which isolate and emphasise the face. In other words in these paintings our attention is concentrated on the individual personality, one might say 'the soul', of the sitter to the virtual exclusion of everything else. It is not that the Trips were poor or even not rich. On the contrary, they were immensely wealthy and powerful, and their huge town mansion, the Trippenhuis, still stands today on the Klovenierzburgwal canal in the Old Centre of Amsterdam. It is that Rembrandt has deliberately chosen to present them this way.

The technical device most characteristic of Rembrandt's portraiture as a whole (though he does not use it in every case), and most associated with his painting as a whole, is a deep chiaroscuro which casts the majority of the picture in shadow while illuminating a small section of the canvas from a single light source. In Rembrandt's hands this device is used to screen out everything which is non-essential while focusing on the psychological or spiritual core of the person or scene that is depicted.[1] The result, again and again, is portrait painting with a degree of personal psychic intensity unprecedented in the history of European and probably world art.

Even more striking evidence of the revolutionary character of Rembrandt's art is afforded by his treatment of the female nude. Let us adopt the same procedure as with the portrait and begin by considering some outstanding examples of the female nude in the European tradition prior to and contemporaneously with Rembrandt. Think of Botticelli's *Birth of Venus* (c1485) (which inaugurated the whole tradition), Giorgione's *Sleeping Venus* (c1510), Titian's *Venus of Urbino* (c1538), Tintoretto's *The Origin of the Milky Way* (c1575-80), Rubens's *The Three Graces* (1639) and, most relevant of all, Velázquez's *The Rokeby Venus* (c1648) (see page 12). In all of these works, without exception, and in innumerable similar paintings pre- and post-Rembrandt, the nude woman is presented as an idealised figure of erotic beauty (as Venus or other mythological figure) posed as an object of display for the male gaze. In short, the woman is presented as an abstract sex object. This tendency, present in all these paintings, reaches an extreme in Velázquez's *Venus*. Despite the brilliance of this work in its handling of colour, depiction of flesh tones and other formal qualities, it is clear that almost every aspect of its composition—the presence of the mirror as a symbol of vanity, the absence of feet, hands and face (except as a very blurred reflection in the mirror),[2] the

2 The tendency to reduce the female nude to an armless and/or headless torso is a feature of the erotic representation of women from the *Venus de Milo* to the photographs of Bill Brandt, the woman thus being rendered 'armless' (pun intended) and mindless.

positioning of the body as a whole with its behind literally in the viewer's face—combines to reduce this image to an impersonal object of desire.

Now look at Rembrandt's *Bathsheba* (1654) (see page 53), painted within a few years of the Velázquez. What a complete contrast! In place of an idealised impersonal body, an actual whole person—a real woman—painted with deep love. It is helpful in looking at this painting to know the bible story on which it is based. King David desired Bathsheba who was married to and pregnant by Uriah. David arranged for Uriah to be sent into battle and killed. The painting depicts the toilet of Bathsheba as she is prepared for the king, whose summons she holds in her right hand. There is thus the potential for intense poignancy built into the scene. However, this is not at all the key factor in shaping the nature and feeling of the painting. In the Amsterdam Rijksmuseum there is a painting of the very same scene, *The Toilet of Bathsheba* (c1594), by Rembrandt's fellow countryman Cornelis Cornelisz van Haarlem (1562-1638) which lacks any of the qualities of the Rembrandt and is much closer, in spirit if not in quality, to Titian or Tintoretto. Of greater significance is the fact that the model for Bathsheba is Hendrickje Stoffels, Rembrandt's lover and companion from about 1650 until her death in

1663, and the strength of his feeling for her is evident in the work. But what is crucial, and what conveys that personal feeling, is the way in which Rembrandt has painted Bathsheba.

This is not easy to express in words. There are compositional elements involved—the presence of, indeed the emphasis on, Bathsheba's feet and hands which works to particularise her, the positioning of her body where she sits straight backed rather than reclining, which conveys strength and dignity. There is the expression on her face, neither coquettish nor pouting nor falsely coy, but an air of deep sadness and resignation entirely appropriate to the situation. There is the peculiarity of her slightly over-long left arm, explanation of which can only be speculative but which I believe is expressive of heaviness and reluctance, which is important because it is symptomatic of Rembrandt painting Bathsheba not from the standpoint of an observer but from, as it were, inside Bathsheba's body.[3] Above all there is the utterly exceptional sensitivity of the handling of the paint in the depiction of every curve, every highlight and every shadow of Bathsheba's body. It is not at all that Rembrandt has given us an asexual or unerotic image of Bathsheba/Hendrickje. On the contrary, it is intensely sexual, suffused with desire, but it is concrete desire for a

3 There is a parallel here with the way in which Michelangelo exaggerates the size of David's right hand as it rests on his thigh, this being the hand that holds the stone that will strike down Goliath.

19

concrete independent woman—desire that can be and is reciprocated, desire that is an integral part of a loving relationship.

It is very hard to overstate how rare an achievement this is in the European art tradition both before and after Rembrandt—only Rubens's study of Helena Fourment as *Venus* (c1636-38) and one or two of Picasso's *Nude in a Red Armchair* paintings of Marie Thérèse Walter come to my mind as in any way similar, and they are plainly not really comparable. Yet it is by no means an isolated or unique example when it comes to Rembrandt's oeuvre. *Woman Bathing in a Stream* (c1654), which hangs in the National Gallery and is also probably modelled for by Hendrickje Stoffels, possesses the same qualities and is equally breathtaking. When one considers the potential for titillation of the pose—the young woman lifting her chemise to the top of her thighs as she steps into the water—it is extraordinary how not an ounce of titillation or voyeurism attaches to this work. Then there is a remarkable series of portraits of Hendrickje, especially *Hendrickje Stoffels Leaning Against a Door* (c1656-57), which has its own particular combination of love, kindliness, strength and independence. Nor are we talking only about images of Hendrickje Stoffels (though clearly she was the most important inspiration in this direction). *The*

Danaë (c1636) in the Hermitage, for whom the model was probably his first wife, Saskia, exhibits a warm, open sexuality that is drawn from the same well.[4] Even Rembrandt's earliest drawings and etchings of anonymous nude women eschew any conventional idealisation or sexualisation.[5] Finally on this theme, there is the etching depicting sexual intercourse called *The French Bed* (1646). In one sense the work is an extremely simple and straightforward naturalistic representation of the sexual act, yet it is also amazing because it manages to be neither biological nor prurient but warm and human. I keep using words like 'amazing', 'exceptional' and 'extraordinary' to describe these paintings because that is what they are. There is simply nothing or almost nothing in the history of European art to compare with them—a sexual but non-sexist representation of nude or semi-nude women.

Portraiture and the nude are by no means the only genres of visual art in which Rembrandt transformed existing modes of representation and, indeed, ways of seeing, as we shall see in the course of this study. Nevertheless, I have already said enough to substantiate my claim regarding the revolutionary nature of Rembrandt's art, and can therefore now move on to the question of how that art came about and what made it possible.

4 Sadly this wonderful painting was all but destroyed when acid was flung at the canvas (the Russian authorities say only that this was done by a 'maniac' and don't reveal or discuss possible motives). Tremendous work has been done to restore the painting, but when I saw it in 1998 I felt its inner light had been extinguished.

5 The only, partial, exception to this that I have found is the early *Andromeda Chained to the Rock* (c1632) in the Mauritshuis, The Hague.

The Anatomy Lesson of Dr Nicolaes Tulp (1632). Mauritshuis, The Hague.

Two Negroes (1661). Mauritshuis, The Hague.

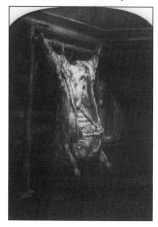

The Night Watch (1642). Rijksmuseum, Amsterdam.
The Slaughtered Ox (1655). Louvre, Paris.

REVOLUTIONARY PORTRAITS

What made Rembrandt's revolutionary art possible? The answer of traditional art history was, and is, Rembrandt's genius. But even if we accept the much debated concept of genius it is clear that this is no real answer. Giotto was a genius. Leonardo was a genius. Why did Giotto's genius and Leonardo's genius produce such different art from Rembrandt's genius? If we explain the nature of Rembrandt's art by the nature of his genius—Rembrandt's genius was for the expression of character and emotion, Monet's genius for conveying impressions of light and colour, that sort of thing—we only push the problem one stage back. What explains the nature of Rembrandt's genius? Of course a kind of answer to this can be given in terms of the artist's personal biography. The way an artist paints is a product of their individual experiences. Obviously there is some truth in this. If an artist loses three children in infancy and his wife in the space of eight years, and then loses his money, his house, then his second great love, and then his one surviving and beloved son—all these things happened to Rembrandt—it is going to affect the way he paints. Nevertheless, there are major problems in placing personal biography at the centre of art historical

6 Charles Fowkes, *The Life of Rembrandt* (London, 1978), is a very useful book, but sometimes falls into this practice, eg, 'Infancy followed a predictable pattern in early 17th century Holland, and we can recreate an accurate picture of Rembrandt's childhood...
Rembrandt's drawings of his own family and their children are the best guide to his childhood.' (pp16-17)

24

explanation. First, we frequently know very few actual facts about an artist's life—this is the case with Rembrandt—and this can lead would-be biographers to write 'constructed' accounts in which gaps in knowledge are filled in by imaginative speculation often on the basis of the art.[6] These imagined 'facts' are then used to analyse the art. Second, the kind of life events that get recorded may not be the life experiences that were the main factors shaping the artist's work. Thirdly, we cannot assume a direct or straightforward relationship between personal experience and art, even when the artists see their work as self-expression and certainly not when they see it quite differently. Finally, the emphasis on personal biography is frequently at the expense of taking into account the influence of society and history in a much wider sense.

One kind of wider influence on which art historians frequently place great emphasis is the influence of other artists past and present. Picasso is analysed in terms of the influence of Cézanne, Gauguin, Matisse, Goya, Velázquez, and so on. For art historians this approach has the obvious advantage of not requiring them to move much beyond their chosen specialism. Also, as with any serious methodology, there is once more an important element of truth here. Every serious artist pays intense attention to the art of their contemporaries and of their predecessors. The most radical modern art always turns out to be nothing more than the next step in an ongoing tradition. But again it is easy and tempting to overemphasise this part of the story.[7] It must be remembered that artists choose their influences. Picasso, had he been or wanted to be a different artist, could have chosen to be influenced by Monet or Renoir instead of Cézanne or Gauguin. Moreover if the artist, like Rembrandt, contributed something genuinely new, then that is precisely what cannot be explained in terms of influences. Once again what is being ignored or downplayed is the influence, direct or indirect, of the wider society.

Sometimes the connection between external social or political developments and particular works of art is so manifest that it cannot be ignored or denied, for example with Picasso's *Guernica* or Goya's *Disasters of War*, but wherever the connection is more subtle or less overt traditional art history tends to turn a blind eye to it. Thus when John Berger suggested that Gainsborough's depiction of *Mr and Mrs Andrews* was bound up with 18th century attitudes to landed property he was met with howls of protest from the art establishment,[8] and when the New York Museum of Modern Art and the Tate Gallery put on their major Jackson Pollock exhibitions in 1998-99 they

7 For an account which tries to explain Rembrandt's transformation of Dutch art primarily in terms of the influence of Italian art of the 16th century, see Kenneth Clarke, *Rembrandt and the Italian Renaissance* (London, 1966).

8 See John Berger, *Ways of Seeing* (London, 1972), pp106-108.

9 For the 'official' view see the exhibition catalogue, Kirk Varnedoe with Pepe Karmel, *Jackson Pollock* (London, 1999), and Jeremy Lewison, *Interpreting Pollock* (London, 1999). For the role of the CIA see Eva Cockroft, 'Abstract Expressionism, Weapon of the Cold War' in Francis Frascina (ed), *Pollock and After: The Critical Debate* (London, 1985). See also my review of the Pollock exhibition, 'Expression of an Age', in *Socialist Review* 229 (April 1999).

10 The list of artists involved in revolutions or attracted by revolutionary or radical ideas is long indeed: Botticelli (with Savonarola in Florence), David, Blake, Courbet, Pissarro, Picasso, Malevich, Léger, Grosz, Rivera, Kahlo, all the Surrealists, to give a small sample from the 15th century to today.

did their best to suppress the Cold War context of Pollock's work, including its cynical promotion by the CIA.[9] Nor is it just a matter of recognising the socio-political dimension—it is how that dimension is interpreted. Traditional art historians are likely to accept, or only be aware of, traditional interpretations of history, and these are likely to seriously underestimate the role of revolutions, revolutionary movements, struggles of the working class and the oppressed, radical ideas, etc (despite the fact that artists themselves are frequently involved with such movements and ideas[10]). For example, all the Impressionists and so called Post-Impressionists lived through an event of immense historical importance and the most horrific brutality, namely the Paris Commune. This involved the working people of Paris seizing control of the city and running it democratically for a period of 74 days until they were crushed by the forces of the Versailles government backed by the Prussian army. In the decisive struggle of the last week central Paris went up in flames and approximately 30,000 Communards were slaughtered in the streets. At the time Monet was 31, Sisley and Cézanne were 32, Gauguin was 23, Van Gogh 18 and Seurat 12. Yet almost none of the accounts of this period or these artists even considers the possible influence of this event on the art of the time.

In 1945 Picasso wrote as follows:

What do you think an artist is? An imbecile who has only his eyes if he's a painter, or ears if he's a musician, or a lyre at every level of his heart if he's a poet, or even if he's a boxer, just his muscles? On the contrary, he's at the same time a political being, constantly alive to heart-rending, fiery or happy events, to which he responds in every way. How would it be possible to feel no interest in other people and by virtue of an ivory indifference to detach yourself from the life which they so copiously bring you? No, painting is not done to decorate apartments. It is an instrument of war for attack and defence against the enemy.[11]

11 Herbert Read, *A Concise History of Modern Painting* (London, 1969), p160.

This statement is not equally true of all artists at all times. It is not even equally true of Picasso at all times. But it is sufficiently true enough of the time for this aspect of the question to merit much more consideration than it usually gets.

When the question is what made a new revolutionary form of art possible, social development in its widest sense, that is not just 'events' but changes in mode of production, social structure and dominant ideology, become especially relevant, for it is changes in these areas which condition at the deepest level how all of us can see and represent the world.

The position I have arrived at here, by means of

an argument beginning from art and art history is, of course, the position that Marx and Engels arrived at in their reflections on the course and dynamic of history—namely that art, like politics, law, religion and philosophy, is part of the superstructure of society, the development of which arises on, and is conditioned by, the economic base or foundation of society.

Apply this position to our question about Rembrandt and the answer is, in a sense, obvious. What made Rembrandt's revolutionary art possible was Dutch society in the first half of the 17th century, and that society was the direct outcome of the Dutch Revolt against rule by the Spanish throne which began in 1566 and resulted in the establishment of the independent Dutch republic.

This revolt is one of the most important but also most underestimated episodes in European history. In the 15th century the geographical area of the Low Countries (today's Belgium, Netherlands and Luxembourg—but in no sense nations at that time) fell under the rule of the dukes of Burgundy, first Philip the Good, then Charles the Bold. When Charles died and his only child, Maria, married Holy Roman Emperor Maximilian I, the area passed into the hands of the Habsburgs and thus by a process of inheritance to Charles V, who was both Holy

Roman Emperor and king of Spain. In 1555 Charles V abdicated and divided his vast territories between his two sons, giving the Holy Roman Empire (much of Germany, Northern Italy, etc) to Ferdinand, and Spain and the Netherlands to Philip. Philip II was a strong proponent of the counter-reformation and determined to suppress the developing Protestant heresy in the Netherlands. A year of famine in 1565 led to a wave of Calvinist iconoclasm (collective destruction of icons in churches), and Philip responded in 1567 by sending the Duke of Alva with an army of 10,000 to crush the rebellion. In the southern Netherlands (including the towns of Ghent, Antwerp and Brussels) the Duke's repression was successful, and this area (today's Belgium) remained under Spanish Habsburg rule. In the north, however, resistance continued under the leadership of William of Orange (known as William the Silent), which resulted in 1579 in the Union of Utrecht which formed the republic of the United Provinces (or Dutch republic) with William of Orange as stadholder or head of state. War with the Spanish throne continued and Dutch independence was only recognised (partially) in the 12-year truce of 1609, three years after Rembrandt's birth, and was not fully confirmed till the Peace of Munster in 1648.

12 J Huizinga, *Dutch Civilisation in the Seventeenth Century* (London, 1968), p112.

What matters for our purposes in this study are not the details of this struggle so much as its general social character and the social character of the society to which it gave rise. This character can only be fully understood from a Marxist perspective, and it is the persistent failure of mainstream historians and art historians to grasp it that accounts for the relative neglect of this period. The point is that the Dutch Revolt was the first fully successful bourgeois revolution and established the first full-blown bourgeois or capitalist state. The designation of 17th century Dutch society and culture as 'bourgeois' is certainly widespread, a cliche indeed, but the term is commonly employed with such imprecision as to deprive it of its main significance and force. For example Johan Huizinga, the eminent Dutch historian, writes:

> *The solidarity of the Dutch people springs from their bourgeois character. Whether we fly high or low, we Dutchmen are all bourgeois—lawyer and poet, baron and labourer alike. Our national culture is bourgeois in every sense you can legitimately attach to that word. The bourgeois conception of life is shared by all classes or groups of our people—urban and rural, property-owning or not. It was from a bourgeois dislike of interference with their affairs that our forefathers rose up against Spain.*[12]

But unless 'bourgeoisie' is understood to refer to a determinate social class defined by its role in the process of production, and bourgeois or capitalist society to signify a specific mode of production characterised by the drive to accumulate capital, then the main point about the Dutch republic is missed, namely its historical novelty. This society in its social structure, its institutions of state and the dynamic of its economy constituted a decisive break with 1,000 years of European feudalism. It was the pioneer of the new form of society, which in the course of the next three centuries was to take over and transform the entire globe.

This is not to suggest that the Dutch republic came out of the blue. Far from it. Rather it was one particular battlefront on the European-wide rise of the bourgeoisie within the framework of feudalism and its struggle against the feudal aristocracy. This development underlay the Italian Renaissance, the German Reformation and the literary flowering of Elizabethan England. Frederick Engels described it as 'the greatest progressive revolution that mankind had so far experienced, a time which called for giants and produced giants', and commented, 'The men who founded the modern rule of the bourgeoisie had anything but bourgeois limitations'.[13] But in the 16th century it was only in

13 Frederick Engels, 'Introduction to Dialectics of Nature' in Karl Marx and Frederick Engels, *Selected Works*, vol 2 (Moscow, 1962), p63. Engels had in mind the likes of Da Vinci, Luther, Dürer and Machiavelli. In this rather neglected essay Engels offers a brief but brilliant synthesis of the economics, politics, culture and science of this epoch.

14 For example one key moment on the struggle was the Siege of Leiden in 1574 which was relieved by opening the dykes and flooding the surrounding area, and it is clearly not accidental that the revolt succeeded in the more inaccessible northern districts beyond.

15 Deric Regin, *Traders, Artists, Burghers: A Cultural History of Amsterdam in the 17th Century* (Amsterdam, 1976), pix.

32

the northern Netherlands that a bourgeois bridgehead was established, to be followed by England in the 1640s. Everywhere else—Spain, Italy, France, Germany, etc— the old order survived, often in the form of triumphant counter-revolution in the guise of the Catholic counter-reformation.

The victory of the Dutch bourgeoisie was the result of a complex combination of circumstances, which ranged from the high level of development of the productive forces in the Netherlands (though at the start of this period these were most advanced in the southern Netherlands round Antwerp where the revolt was defeated) to the unique topography of the area,[14] to the exceptionally tangled international situation which ensured that, although Philip II's military forces were more than capable of crushing the forces of William of Orange, Philip found himself compelled to fight on many fronts at once (against the Turks, the Barbary Corsairs, the revolt of the Moriscos in Granada, the English, the French, etc) and consequently ran out of funds to pay his army in the low countries. But whatever the causes of the success of the Dutch Revolt, its outcome, and this is what is most important, for understanding Rembrandt, was, in the words of Dutch poet and historian Deric Regin, 'the development of the first autonomous bourgeois culture in modern history'.[15]

Key features of Dutch society

16 Immanuel Wallerstein, *The Modern World System: II* (New York, 1980), pp38-39.

The most obvious and fundamental characteristic of this new society was its exceptional economic dynamism and prosperity. The designation of this period in Dutch history as 'the golden age' does of course take cognisance of the magnificent art of the time, but it refers first and foremost to the huge fortunes amassed by the country's traders, bankers and manufacturers. The Dutch republic was the Japan of the 17th century, and nothing underlines its spectacular progress so clearly as the contrast between its development and that of the southern Netherlands. As we have already noted, prior to the rebellion it was the south—Antwerp and its environs— that was most economically advanced. In the 17th century the north, liberated from the fetters of Habsburg rule, leapt forward while the south entered a long period of stagnation and decline.

Immanuel Wallerstein waxes lyrical about the United Provinces as 'the hegemonic power of the capitalist world economy', claiming that it was able to 'manifest simultaneously productive, commercial and financial superiority over all other core powers'.[16]

Not only did the Dutch dominate the North Sea herring fishery, but they dominated the Iceland cod

17 Ibid, p39.
18 Ibid, p42.
19 Ibid, p43.
20 Ibid, p44.
21 Ibid, p46.
22 Ibid, p58.

34

fishery and the Spitzbergen whale fishery as well.[17]

The United Provinces not only was the leading agricultural producer of this time. It was also, and at the same time, the leading producer of industrial products. Over a 100-year period, industrial production of textiles surged forward and it reached a peak in the 1660s (an index calculated for 1664 is 545 as compared with 100 for 1584 and 108 for 1795).[18]

The second great industry of early modern times was shipbuilding, and here too the lead of the United Provinces is common knowledge.[19]

Holland was a leading centre of sugar refining, at least in 1660.[20] Dutch shipping dominated the world carrying trade. As of 1670 the Dutch owned three times the tonnage of the English, and more than the tonnage of England, France, Portugal, Spain and the Germanies combined.[21]

In 1609, the Year of the Truce, De Wisselbank van Amsterdam was founded. It quickly became the great centre of European deposit and exchange.[22]

One consequence of this economic dynamism—an especially remarkable one when one looks back with 20th century eyes accustomed to the examples of Germany, Italy and other late developing capitalist powers—was that in the space of a single generation the

United Provinces not only emerged as an independent state but became a world colonial power. Sea power was at the heart of Dutch prosperity from the start and played a central role in the struggle against Habsburg rule. The 60 or so years following the foundation of the Dutch East India Company in 1602—years that coincide almost exactly with the life of Rembrandt—saw the Dutch use that sea power to establish outposts of their empire from the Moluccas (Indonesia) and Japan in the Far East to New Amsterdam (Manhattan) and Pernambuco (north east Brazil) in the West, and from Spitzbergen in the far north to Cape Town in the far south. Thus for all its supposed 'bourgeois moderation' the Dutch Republic played a pioneering role in the brutal process Marx called the primitive accumulation of capital, which ensured that if money came into the world with 'a congenital blood-stain on one cheek, capital comes dripping from head to foot, from every pore, with blood and dirt'.[23]

Another remarkable feature of the Netherlands was the degree of its urbanisation. To put this in perspective, it should be noted that 50 percent of the British population lived in towns only in 1850, ie after the industrial revolution, and in this Britain led the world, with the US and Russia reaching the same landmark only in the 20th

23 Karl Marx, *Capital*, vol I (London, 1974), pp711-712.

24 Jonathan Israel, *The Dutch Republic: Its Rise, Greatness and Fall* (Oxford, 1995), p115.
25 Ibid, p115.
26 See tables, ibid, p328 and p621.

century. Holland, however (the province of Holland, not the Netherlands as a whole), was already roughly half urban as early as 1550.[24] In 1550 the north Netherlands (to become the Dutch republic) had 11 cities over 10,000 compared with only four in the much larger Britain.[25] This already well established urban concentration was greatly accelerated by the success of the Dutch Revolt. By 1600 the number of towns over 10,000 rose to 19 and each of these towns itself grew rapidly. Amsterdam went from 30,000 in 1570 to 60,000 in 1600, 140,000 in 1647 and 200,000 in 1672. Leiden (Rembrandt's birthplace) over the same period grew from 15,000 to 72,000, Haarlem from 16,000 to 50,000, and Rotterdam from 7,000 to 45,000.[26]

The driving force of this growth was not natural increase (an excess of births over deaths) but immigration. Jonathan Israel explains:

In early modern times, urban growth, even to a modest extent, let alone the kind of spectacular expansion which occurred in Holland…was possible only through high levels of immigration…from rural areas within the country or from abroad… For in all early modern cities, including those of the Dutch Golden Age, the death rate appreciably exceeded the birth rate… Heavy infant mortality, combined with epidemics, especially of plague (until the 1660s) ensured a built in excess of deaths over births... Consequently, rapid urban growth in early modern times…was a more impressive and astounding phenomenon than it would be in a more recent context.[27]

27 Ibid, pp328-329.
28 Ibid, p115.

The main sources of immigration were, first, the southern Netherlands, followed by Protestant Germany and the eastern rural provinces of the republic. The push factors were Spanish repression in the south, the Thirty Years War in Germany, and rural poverty. The pull factor was the dynamism and prosperity of the Dutch economy. The precise role of the Dutch Revolt in this process is tellingly illustrated in the population statistics for the north and south Netherlands. In 1550, before the revolt, the south had 360,000 people in cities over 10,000 to the north's 182,000. In 1600, after the revolt, the south had only 250,000 to the north's 365,000.[28] In short, in the first half of the 17th century the Dutch republic was the most urbanised society in the world, and what made it so was its revolution.

The Dutch republic also led the world at this time in terms of tolerance and freedom of the individual, and once again this was directly attributable to the revolution. In the 17th century tolerance meant first and foremost religious tolerance. Svetlana Alpers writes with a certain retrospective awe of 'the extraordinary lack of

29 Svetlana Alpers, *The Art of Describing: Dutch Art in the Seventeenth Century* (Chicago, 1983), pxxvi.

30 Even Simon Schama recognises this: 'Dutch patriotism was not the cause but the consequence of the revolt against Spain.' Simon Schama, *The Embarrassment of Riches* (London, 1988), p69.

31 Frederick Engels, *Socialism: Utopian and Scientific* (Peking, 1975), p26.

38

religious prejudice or aggression in Holland…compared to the rest of Europe', and, somewhat at a loss, observes that 'Dutchmen seem to have suffered much less than other Europeans from a sense of the threat posed by conflicting views of society or of God'.[29] However, if it is grasped that the fundamental driving force of the Dutch Revolt was class, not religion or nationalism (Dutch nationalism was a considerable force but it was the outcome, not the cause, of the revolt[30]), there is no great mystery. In the years of the revolt it was the Calvinists who played the leading part, taking the role, in a manner that foreshadowed the Jacobins of 1793 and the Bolsheviks of 1917, of the 'vanguard' of the revolution. It was a role for which their faith and organisation were well suited. As Engels noted:

> *Calvin's creed was one fit for the boldest of the bourgeoisie of his time… Calvin's church constitution was thoroughly democratic and republican: and where the kingdom of God was republicanised, could the kingdoms of this world remain subject to monarchs, bishops and lords? While German Lutheranism became a willing tool in the hands of princes, Calvinism founded a republic in Holland, and active republican parties in England and, above all, Scotland.*[31]

But the Calvinists, like other vanguards, were a minority, at first a very small minority. One estimate suggests that in 1587 they constituted only one tenth of the population,[32] and another that by 1672 they were one third.[33] In addition to Calvinists there were Lutherans, Anabaptists, Mennonites, Jews, probably some atheists and, importantly, a significant proportion of Catholics. The need for unity in the struggle against Habsburg rule thus dictated a policy of religious toleration. It could not be pure tolerance, for the Dutch revolutionaries had to reckon with the fact that the Roman Catholic church was the principal international institution of feudal counter-revolution and that, therefore, its dominant position had to be destroyed. But for ordinary Catholics freedom of conscience was maintained so as not to force them into the arms of Spain. Tolerance for Catholics meant a degree of tolerance for everyone else (including Jews),[34] and tolerance in the religious sphere spilled over into the spheres of politics, philosophy and science. J L Price describes the scene as follows:

To the modern mind the Dutch republic…is remarkable chiefly for the great school of painting it produced… For contemporaries…the distinctive and surprising feature of Dutch 17th century society was the remarkable degree of freedom of thought and belief which it allowed…no other state in Europe…was able, or wished, to grant its subjects so much freedom—of conscience, of speech, and, in practice, of the

32 Geoffrey Parker, *The Dutch Revolt* (London, 1977), p154.

33 Ibid, p241.

34 The precise terms and limits of this tolerance were the subject of much vigorous debate and contention in the course of the 17th century. See Jonathan Israel, op cit, pp499-505 and pp637-644.

39

35 J L Price, *Culture and Society in the Dutch Republic During the 17th Century* (London, 1974), pp170-171.

36 Prior to the women's movement of the 1960s and 1970s only the Russian Revolution of 1917 had attempted to establish both legal and real social equality for women, and this heroic endeavour soon foundered on lack of resources before it was rolled back by Stalinism.

press… In addition, the republic became a haven for those who would have been, or had been, persecuted in their own countries for their opinions... Original and daring thinkers knew that they were less likely to be harassed as a result of their speculation...than elsewhere.[35]

As a result John Lilburne the English Leveller, Descartes, Spinoza, Locke and Boyle all, at one time or another, found it necessary or congenial to avail themselves of the benefits of Dutch freedom in the Golden Age.

One aspect of Dutch society of particular significance for our subject is the relative status of women. It is difficult to be precise or concrete on this. When one remembers that neither the French nor the American revolutions granted women even legal equality, and that even the Paris Commune of 1871 failed to give women the vote, it is clear that there could be no question of women's liberation or equality in the modern sense.[36] Nevertheless it is also clear that by the standards of the time and in comparison with the position of women in neighbouring countries Dutch women were relatively strong, independent and emancipated.

No aspect of Dutch freedom in the Golden Age struck contemporaries, especially foreigners, more than that enjoyed by women—of all classes and types. Dutch women, even young unmarried women, were free to come and go, unaccompanied and unchaperoned, to work, conduct business and engage in conversation almost like men. Everyone agreed that in Dutch society wives were less subservient to their husbands than elsewhere.[37]

The Italian observer Gregorio Leti 'claimed that wife beating was uncommon in Holland because neighbours would not tolerate it...[and that] it was unacceptable to slap servants with or without other people present as was usual, for example, in France'.[38] Also worth noting is that 'the Dutch Republic was one of the first countries to put a stop to the execution of witches',[39] the last being in 1597.

All this liberality and tolerance had its limits, however. It did not, for example, extend to beggars, of whom there were many (as a result of basic poverty, fluctuations of the market, and injury and disablement at sea and in the wars with Spain). The Protestant work ethic was, of course, very strong among the Dutch burghers, and begging was regarded by them as a social problem, a sin and a crime. Captured beggars were variously whipped, branded, put in the pillory, set to forced labour in the galleys, imprisoned and banished. It is evidently an extreme case, but van Deursen gives us the example of

37 Jonathan Israel, op cit, p677.

38 Cited ibid, p678.

39 A T van Deursen, *Plain Lives in a Golden Age* (Cambridge, 1991), p252.

40 Ibid, p50.
41 Ibid, p57.
42 Karl Marx, op cit, p686.
43 Ibid, p688.

42

'Trijn Pieters from Maasluis [who] was banned ten times between 1606 and 1617, the year of her execution…[and] who over time carried the marks of four brandings on her body, and from 1612 was recognisable by her cut off ears'.[40] (Van Deursen also makes clear that in practice ordinary people took a very different view from the authorities, quoting Samuel Coster's poetic reference to 'the people's great mercy/For the needy and in particular for the foreign poor', and commenting, 'Anyone who belonged to the brotherhood of the poor knew he had much in common with the beggar'.[41])

The persecution of beggars was not accidental. In volume one of *Capital* Marx documents the 'bloody legislation against vagabondage'[42] throughout Western Europe in the early modern period, giving examples from England, France and the Netherlands, and sums it up as follows:

Thus were the agricultural people, first forcibly expropriated from the soil, driven from their homes, turned into vagabonds and then whipped, branded, tortured by laws grotesquely terrible, into the discipline necessary for the wage system.[43]

Nor was the treatment of beggars an isolated question. It was closely linked to two other aspects of Dutch society—the treatment of offenders and the treatment of the poor. 'Justice in 17th century Holland', writes Charles Fowkes, 'was simple and remorseless'.[44] By the very unpleasant standards of the day the United Provinces were not especially sadistic but they had their share of severe punishments—flogging, branding, mutilation and various forms of execution, including death by drowning.[45] It was a society which placed a high value on order and discipline and which, through institutions such as the Amsterdam House of Correction, vividly described by Simon Schama,[46] was perhaps a pioneer of that transition, noted by Michel Foucault,[47] from a state maintaining itself by public displays of vengeance on the bodies of malefactors to a regime of minute surveillance and control exemplified by the panopticon (Bentham's prison designed so that a single warder could survey every prisoner in every cell at all times).

With regard to poverty, it is always difficult to establish precise cross-cultural and trans-historical comparisons. Jonathan Israel maintains strongly, and persuasively, that the booming Dutch economy paid wages 'higher than were to be found elsewhere in Western Europe', and that 'after 1590, the north Netherlands became the only part of Europe where wages rose faster than the cost of living'.[48] But it is no less true that the greatly enhanced wealth of Dutch society was distributed

44 Charles Fowkes, op cit, p46.

45 Simon Schama, op cit, pp25-26.

46 Ibid, pp15-24.

47 See Michel Foucault, *Discipline and Punish: The Birth of the Prison* (Harmondsworth 1977).

48 Jonathan Israel, op cit, pp351-352.

49 J Bolten and H Bolten-Rempt, *The Hidden Rembrandt* (Oxford, 1978), p8.
50 Charles Fowkes, op cit, p18.
51 A T van Deursen, op cit, pp5-7.
52 Jonathan Israel, op cit, pp353-355.
53 Ibid, p355.

extremely unequally. Bolten and Bolten-Rempt put it simply: '...in contrast to a prosperous bourgeoisie, the mass of people was very badly off'.[49] Fowkes writes of the slums of Leiden where the young Rembrandt 'would have seen the other face of nascent bourgeois capitalism, when profiteer landlords exploited Leyden's 20,000 textile workers who dragged out their existence in rotting, barrack-like hovels'.[50] And van Deursen, in a careful analysis of wages and bread prices, shows that, despite a working day beginning at 4am or 5am, and lasting to between 7pm and 9pm, large numbers of workers were frequently unable to afford enough bread to sustain their families and so officially became paupers.[51]

For these very numerous paupers there was, Israel observes, an 'elaborate system of civic poor relief and charitable institutions' which 'regularly amazed'[52] foreigners by its efficiency. However, as Israel also tells us, 'some of the major motives' behind these welfare provisions 'were in fact quite far removed from those of compassion',[53] in that a major concern was the maintenance of strict discipline and social control. On the real nature of this poor relief and the relations between the class that administered it and the class that received it we have two remarkable, if unusual, pieces of historical evidence—the two group portraits by the aged Frans Hals, himself a pauper, of the *Regents and Regentesses of the Old Men's Alms House in Haarlem* in 1664. These great paintings testify in the clearest possible terms to the mutual hatred and contempt involved in this early example of bourgeois charity.[54]

To speak of beggars, of crime and punishment, and of the poor, is to remind ourselves that although this was a revolutionary society it was also a capitalist one. Being a capitalist society meant that the economic growth, though spectacular, was not smooth or regular. It proceeded, as it has done in capitalism ever since, through great forward surges followed by setbacks, through the alternation of booms and slumps. In particular there was the great tulip mania of 1636-37. Tulips were first brought to the Netherlands from Turkey in the 16th century and started out as a luxury import for the aristocracy. But, of course, they were reproducible, and as their cultivation developed in Holland their popularity spread among the middle and lower middle classes. Gradually tulip bulbs became objects of speculation.

Investments in trade were often made for short periods. The tulip by its nature was well suited to this. Freshly planted bulbs could be sold straight away with the promise of delivery of flowers the following summer. Before they were in bloom, they could be resold

54 An analysis of these paintings and a critique of their normal treatment in traditional art history form a key passage in John Berger, *Ways of Seeing*, op cit, pp11-16. Berger comments, 'Hals was the first portraitist to paint the new characters and expressions created by capitalism.' He also writes, 'They [the paintings] work upon us because we accept the way Hals saw his sitters... We accept it in so far as it corresponds to our own observation of people, gestures, faces, institutions. This is possible because we still live in a society of comparable social relations and moral values. And it is precisely this which gives the paintings their psychological and social urgency.'

45

55 A T van Deursen, op cit, p68.
56 Ibid, p69.
57 Ibid, p70.

many times.[55]

Then in 1636 the speculation assumed a frenzied character. Prices went through the roof, multiplying by the hour and the day. People gave up work to buy and sell tulips, and 'tulips were traded for a coach and horses, for cows, for fur coats and for paintings'.[56] In February 1637 the speculative market collapsed. 'A few people had become rich, and many poor'.[57]

Just as the United Provinces' tremendous economic growth, urbanisation and liberalism testify to this society's revolutionary break with the prevailing European order, so its treatment of beggars and paupers, and its feverish pursuit of profit testify to its contradictory character, and link it to the present day—to the persecution of refugees, Gypsies and beggars in Blair's Britain, and to the internet bubble of the year 2001.

Dutch society and Dutch art

Such was the society that produced Rembrandt. But
Rembrandt did not stand alone. He was merely the foremost of a multitude of artists who between them ensured
that the most spectacular and lasting legacy of the
Golden Age was its visual art. St Luke, the patron saint
of painters, is not a supporter of devolution. Despite the
complaints of provincials, the history of Western art
shows again and again the tendency of its finest expo-
nents to emerge and/or to congregate in certain cities
and regions—Florence, Venice, Paris, Berlin, New York,
London, and so on. In the 17th century it was the cities
of the Dutch republic—Delft, Haarlem and, above all,
Amsterdam—that were the focus of a spectacular flowering of art including such names as Frans Hals, Jacob van
Ruisdael, Pieter de Hooch, Jan Stein, Adriaen Brouwer,
Carel Fabritius, Ferdinand Bol, Aelbert Cuyp, Meindert
Hobbema and Jan Vermeer.

Before returning to our principal subject it is
necessary to consider briefly some of the main characteristics of Dutch art and their relationship to the Dutch
social order.

The first contribution of the Dutch Revolt to
Dutch art was a negative one—the elimination of the

58 By devotional art I do not mean religious art, which continued, but art designed to assist worship in churches.

59 J L Price, op cit, p64.

60 Charles Fowkes, op cit, p1.

61 S Alpers, *The Art of Describing: Dutch Art in the Seventeenth Century* (London, 1983), pxxv.

48

leading cultural role of the Roman Catholic church, and of the court and aristocracy. These three social forces which had dominated European painting for centuries were suddenly marginalised. This meant the rapid disappearance of devotional art:[58] no more great altarpieces, no more Sistine Chapels or church frescoes. It meant no more vast mythological canvases adorning palace walls, no more monumental spirals of entwined flesh à la Rubens, no more swagger portraits à la Van Dyck. In their place came a massive expansion of the market for art among the bourgeoisie and petty bourgeoisie:

With the great patrons of the past absent…the cultural life of the republic was dominated by the middle and upper classes in the towns of Holland. The painters formed their market partly among the regent elite but more largely in a wide section of the town population—not only the rich, but those sections of the population with money to spend, or rather invest, in works of art.[59]

Charles Fowkes may possibly be exaggerating when he speaks of 'the greatest popular demand for "art" in history',[60] but it is clear that Svetlana Alpers is right that 'in Holland the visual culture was central to the life of the society'.[61] Foreign visitors expressed their amazement at the number of paintings they encountered on their travels:

62 English traveller Peter Mundy cited in C Fowkes, op cit, p22.
63 *The Diary of John Evelyn*, cited ibid, p42.
64 S Alpers, op cit, pxxii.

...As for the art off painting and the affection of the people to pictures, I thincke none other goe beyond them... All in generall stirring to adorne their houses, especially the outer street roome, with costly peeces.[62]

...We arrived late at Roterdam, where was at that time their annual Mart or Faire, so furnish'd with pictures...as I was amazed... The reason of this store of pictures and their cheapness proceede from their want of Land, to employ their stock; so as 'tis an ordinary thing to find, a common Farmer lay out two, or 3000 pounds this commodity, their houses are full of them.[63]

Some major works, like Rembrandt's *The Night Watch*, were commissioned by civic authorities, regents and corporate boards, but huge amounts were produced for the market, and Alpers makes an interesting comparison with the present:

From the point of view of its consumption, art as we think of it in our time in many respects began with Dutch art. Its societal role was not far from that of art today; a liquid investment like silver, tapestries or other valuables, pictures were bought from artists' shops or on the open market as possessions, and hung, one presumes, to fill space and to decorate domestic walls. We have few records of commissions and little evidence of buyers' demands.[64]

Clearly this meant many small paintings rather

65 Kenneth Clark, *An Introduction to Rembrandt* (London, 1978), p63.
66 Charles Wilson, *The Dutch Republic* (London, 1968), p119.
67 H Knackfuss, *Rembrandt* (Bielefeld and Leipzig, 1899), p2.

than a few or medium number of very large ones. But the economic and social base of the Dutch republic conditioned the content and style of Dutch art as well as its quantity and size. Svetlana Alpers's book on the 17th century is entitled *The Art of Describing*, and most commentators seem to agree. Kenneth Clark writes, 'Never has capitalism shown a rosier face than in the Amsterdam of the 1630s and, as usually happens in the first expansions of bourgeois culture, people wanted to have their appearances perpetuated by art',[65] and Charles Wilson writes that 'it was the triumph of Holland's painters that they succeeded in depicting the ordinary things of everyday life with a passionate intensity that has never been surpassed'.[66] Indeed this view was well established a century ago, as we can see from this 1899 observation:

> *The task to which the new nation set its artists is put very well in the words of a French writer: 'It wanted its picture painted.' That is, in truth, what Dutch painting amounts to: the honest truthful picture of country, people and things, the rendering of the simple facts of the home and of everyday life.*[67]

Thus we arrive at the principal genres of Dutch painting—maritime paintings including paintings of sea battles à la van de Velde the younger, reflecting the dependence of the republic on sea power and the role of the navy in the revolt; landscapes of unprecedented naturalism depicting the flat, orderly, peopled Dutch countryside[68] (none of Claude's grand classical pastorals or Turner's untamed forces of nature); domestic interiors of sublime precision redolent of modest prosperity and respectability; scenes of everyday living including the picturesque low-life; still lifes including flower paintings of some passion, lobsters you feel you can eat, 'the edible made visible',[69] and, for amusement on the side, superb *trompe l'oeiles*; intimate pious religious scenes for moral edification and consolation; above all, portraits and group portraits in spectacular numbers so that 'proportionately more faces were captured in a variety of ways in the Netherlands than in any other country in the 17th century',[70] perhaps ever, before photography.

All of this can be seen, and often has been seen, as a simple reflection of the everyday lives of the Dutch middle classes for whose walls it was destined. In reality painting is never simple photographic reflection (neither is photography), and there is no unproblematic or neutral realism. As so often, it is John Berger who sharpens the argument and puts his finger on the key issue:

The art of any period tends to serve the ideological interests of the ruling class… What is being proposed is a little more precise; that a way of seeing the world, which was

68 In my opinion the emergence of Dutch landscape painting, 'the first pure landscapes' according to John Berger (op cit, p105), was a response to and therefore bound up with the dramatic urbanisation of Dutch society as much as Constable's landscapes and Romantic nature poetry were a response to the industrialisation and urbanisation of Britain. I therefore do not agree with Berger that Dutch landscapes 'answered no direct social need.' (Ibid, p105)

69 Ibid, p99.

70 Ernst van de Wetering, 'The Multiple Functions of Rembrandt's Self-Portraits' in Christopher White and Quentin Buvelot (eds), *Rembrandt by Himself*, (London, 1999), p10. Van de Wetering continues, 'Dr Ekkart has estimated that 50,000 (approximately 1.5 percent) of the 3 million people who populated the northern Netherlands over three generations probably had their portraits painted!'

71 John Berger, op cit, pp86-87.

ultimately determined by new attitudes to property and exchange, found its visual expression in the oil painting, and could not have found it in any other visual art form.

Oil painting did to appearances what capital did to social relations. It reduced everything to the equality of objects. Everything became exchangeable because everything became a commodity. All reality was mechanically measured by its materiality.[71]

Berger is writing about the tradition of oil painting as a whole, but that does not stop his words applying with particular force to Dutch art of the 17th century, provided we also bear in mind that the revolutionary novelty of Dutch society lent its art, even its middling art, a certain austerity and freshness not available to most European oil painting at other times.

Bathsheba (1654). Louvre, Paris.

Beggar Seated on a Bank (1630). Rijksmuseum, Amsterdam.

De Staalmeesters (1662). Rijksmuseum, Amsterdam.

54

One-Legged Beggar (1634). British Museum, London.

The Return of the Prodigal Son (1668), Hermitage. St Petersburg.

REVOLUTIONARY PORTRAITS

Rembrandt as bourgeois artist

So where does Rembrandt stand in relation to Dutch art and Dutch society? In some respects he is its supreme representative, the bourgeois artist par excellence.

Born in Leiden, the ninth son of a miller and his relatively prosperous wife, his background was classically petty bourgeois, the typical class position of the artist under capitalism.[72] His talent showed itself early, and by the age of 20 he was established as an independent painter. At 23 he was spotted by a man of power, Constantijn Huygens, secretary to Stadholder Frederik Henry, and by his late twenties he was a highly successful, probably the most successful, painter in Amsterdam. Judging by his output at the beginning of his career Rembrandt's original intention was to be a history painter, ie a painter of action scenes from the Bible and classical mythology (traditionally regarded as the highest form of painting). Approximately two thirds of his known paintings from the period 1625-29 are history paintings. Thereafter, roughly coinciding with his recognition by Huygens, the proportion of history paintings declines abruptly to about one in five, remaining roughly at that level for the rest of his life. Instead Rembrandt turned to portrait painting, and portraits (including group portraits

72 Impressionistic evidence suggests that in the capitalist epoch most artists came from a middle to lower middle class background (though in the 20th century there has also been a significant working class minority coming through the art colleges), but it is important to understand that the objective class position of the large majority of artists, whatever their background, is petty bourgeois in that predominantly they are self-employed or small employers selling, not their labour power, but the products of their labour where possible to the rich.

55

73 These figures are very rough because many of Rembrandt's works blur the categories (for example his 'portraits' of Christ or his 1651 'portrait' of King David) and because of arguments about attribution, but I am only interested in the general trend, which is clear.

and self-portraits) make up two thirds or more of his subsequent work.[73] Of these a substantial proportion, and the main means by which Rembrandt earned his very considerable living, were commissions to paint portraits or group portraits of members of the Dutch bourgeoisie, and for the most part these were paintings which the clients would have been pleased to receive.

This does not mean that these were inferior or hack works. On the contrary, most of them are extremely good of their kind, executed with exemplary technical skill and acute psychological insight. Let us take for example the 1634 portrait of *Maerten Soolmans* (one of a typical marriage pair with wife Oopjen Coppit). Soolmans is clearly a fashionable man about town and flashy dresser. Rembrandt makes this the occasion for a *tour de force* of lace painting, particularly with regard to the outrageous rosettes on Soolmans's shoes. There is, one suspects, a slight element of irony or mockery in Rembrandt's portrayal of this self-satisfied young man, but it is unlikely that a man who could wear such rosettes would detect it. Rembrandt produced many such society portraits and they are far from being his greatest work. Nevertheless, besides exceptional naturalistic and verisimilitude technique they also usually have built into them an inner dynamism or movement in the pose and the contrast of light and dark which distinguishes them from the average rather wooden portrait of the day.

An outstanding example of these qualities is *The Anatomy Lesson of Dr Nicolaes Tulp* (1632) (see page 22). It is clear that the group portrait had a special place in the culture of the ascendant Dutch bourgeoisie—Schutterij (paintings of militia companies like *The Night Watch*), regents of almshouses and charitable boards, (like the aforementioned works by Hals), burgomasters and guild-masters, surgeons' anatomy lessons. All these were established conventions of Dutch painting. In them the Dutch burghers sought to find themselves reflected as strong, confident, united, moral, dignified, learned, austere, the epitome of whatever Protestant and bourgeois virtues were appropriate for the role and occasion. It is also clear that Rembrandt's *Anatomy Lesson* exists within these conventions. It was his first commission for a large group portrait, indeed one of his first commissions of any kind, and it seems likely that he wished to please his clients, the Amsterdam Guild of Surgeons. Yet the painting is a masterpiece of social and psychological observation—each surgeon so similar but different—and of formal composition. The angle of each head and each hand, the line of each nose and point of each beard, the light on each forehead and each ruff forms a living pyramid looming over the pallid laid-out corpse and its red flayed arm. The subject matter of the painting allows for much speculative interpretation regarding 'the body as text', the social role of surgeons and science, the development of anatomical knowledge and the treatment of criminals (the body is that of Adriaen Adriaensze, known as 'the child', a hanged criminal). But this is secondary to my point, which is that, despite the fact that the painting lacks 'soul' or intensity of feeling and is basically a publicity painting, it still puts most group portraits of the time, or any other time, in the shade by virtue of its inner dynamism.

On those occasions when Rembrandt finds something genuinely admirable or moving in his sitters he achieves even greater wonders within the framework of the commissioned portrait. The marvellous portraits of *Jacob Trip* and *Margaretha de Geer* discussed at the beginning of this study fall into this category, though they break with some of its conventions. So does the extraordinary *Staalmeesters* or *The Sampling Officials of the Drapers' Guild* (1662) (see page 54). This has all the merits of *The Anatomy Lesson* raised to a higher level, to virtual perfection. The arrangement of the six figures round the table is apparently natural and straightforward but in reality is a masterpiece of subtle calculation designed to bring the whole group to life as a differentiated totality.

The miraculously painted red tablecloth bathes the whole canvas in warm light. And for all their evident dignity and stature Rembrandt captures the hardness in the sampling officials' characters required for their role but, as with the portrait of *Maerten Soolmans*, with so deft a touch that men of such character could hardly take offence. In my opinion it is the greatest painting of its genre in history.

Two other examples of this kind are the portraits of *The Amsterdam Merchant Nicolaes Ruts* (1631) and *Jan Six* (1654). *The Staalmeesters* is the work of an ageing master, displaying all his accumulated craft. The *Nicolaes Ruts* is work of a young virtuoso—Rembrandt was only 25—but it still shows great maturity as well as brilliant technique. If the technique is seen in the rendering of the velvet hat and fur coat, it is first and foremost the pose—the grip of the right hand, the slight forward inclination of the body, the hint of the braced shoulders, the angle of the head across the body, the implied statement or question in the left hand holding the note—which lends the figure its dynamism. This is complemented by the facial expression, with its clear piercing eyes. As Simon Schama has pointed out, the fur also tells an interesting story:

> For *Nicolaes Ruts is literally wearing his stock in*

74 Simon Schama, *Rembrandt's Eyes* (London, 1999), pp334-335. This is a huge and, in my opinion, very ill judged book on Rembrandt (which I have reviewed very critically), but Schama's detailed knowledge enables him to make a number of useful observations about particular paintings.

75 Ibid, p337.

trade: sable. *No fabric of any kind—not Persian silk, not Indian calico, not French-worked damask—was more precious than sable…the fur that was used by the Muscovite Tsars as diplomatic gifts and treaty-sweeteners… And yet for all the unparalleled magnificence of the coat that sits on the shoulders of the fur trader, Rembrandt has managed to avoid the least impression of vanity or idle opulence… He is the epitome of the entrepreneur-as-man-of-action—not a complete fiction, since the Muscovy fur trade [out of Arkhangelisk] was certainly one of the more heroically risky of the 'fine' trades.*[74]

Schama goes on to say it is no wonder that the painting was later bought by J P Morgan since there has never been 'a better portrait of the businessman as hero'.[75]

Jan Six, who was for a period Rembrandt's friend, was an even richer and more prominent merchant than Ruts. Six inherited his wealth from his grandfather's textile business, and retired from business in 1652 to devote himself to poetry, art collecting and various state duties, serving as maritime commissioner in 1659 and mayor of Amsterdam in 1691. He was without doubt one of the most distinguished representatives of the Dutch ruling class in the Golden Age. Yet Rembrandt's portrait of him is distinguished by its extremely effective combination of bright colours (red, yellow and grey), and even more so by the exceptional freedom and looseness of the brushwork, especially on the hands, the buttons and the scarlet cloak with its yellow braid. In its handling of paint the portrait looks forward to Goya, 150 years later, and even Manet, 200 years later.

But the point is that this was an age in which a painter of Rembrandt's sensitivity could paint a business-man as hero and a member of the ruling class in the manner of Goya or Manet without satirising him, and not just because the voyage to Arkhangelisk was fraught with peril or because Jan Six was a man of taste, but because the Dutch bourgeoisie were the makers and products of a heroic revolution. It was not an age that was to last long.

This history of art shows that there are periods when certain kinds of paintings are possible and then periods when they cease to be possible. If one compares Piero della Francesca's *Baptism of Christ by St John the Baptist* or his *Resurrection* with Stanley Spencer's *Resurrection in Cookham*, or Mathias Grünewald's *Crucifixion* with Salvador Dali's *Christ of St John of the Cross*, it is clear that the time of great Christian art is over and cannot be restored by any act of will. Velázquez could produce a masterpiece like his *Pope Innocent X.* For Francis Bacon to make serious art of this material it had to come out as *Screaming Pope.* Holbein could paint a great portrait of *Henry VIII.* All recent portraits of British royalty are complete rubbish. The era when a great artist could paint a great portrait of a businessman or ruler did not last long and came to a definitive end in the mid-19th century, about the time of the 1848 revolutions. Jacques Louis David, who during the French Revolution voted for the death of Louis XVI, could glorify Napoleon in *Napoleon Crossing the Alps* (1805). Picasso, despite being a member of the Communist Party and willing to try, could do nothing with Stalin.

Rembrandt was the supreme bourgeois artist, not only in his portraits of the Dutch bourgeoisie, but also in his portraits of himself. Many artists—Dürer, Titian, Rubens, etc—produced individual self-portraits before Rembrandt, but never in such numbers. Rembrandt produced more than 70, and he produced them at every stage of his career. For no artist before Rembrandt, and none after until Van Gogh, was the self-portrait so central to their output. Nearly all these self-portraits were displayed in a magnificent exhibition at the National Gallery in 1999. In an unparalleled visual documentation of a life they recorded Rembrandt's passage from brilliant prodigy to mature master to broken—or is it unbroken—old man. Together they constitute one of the wonders of world culture, taking further, almost to the limit imaginable, the visual representation of personality, of 'self' or of 'soul', that we have already noted at the beginning of this study as a distinctive and revolutionary feature of Rembrandt's art, and which also corresponds to one of the key social and intellectual themes of the rise of the bourgeois epoch, namely the rise of the individual and of individualism.

In *Rembrandt by Himself*, the book accompanying the National Gallery exhibition, this view is rejected. Ernst van de Wetering, in the keynote article, argues that 'the prevailing view of the self-portrait as a means for "self-examination" is an anachronism when applied to the period before 1800',[76] because the notion of the 'self' to be explored dates only from the Romantic period (roughly the French Revolution and its aftermath) and was not available to Rembrandt in the 17th century. Instead van de Wetering attributes the proliferation of self-portraits to 'the strength of the demand from collectors for these works...which were seen as representative of his art and of the techniques for which he was most famous.[77] This argument links Rembrandt's self-portraits to the rise of capitalism via the art market and the demand of 'consumers' rather than via the consciousness of the artist, and I see no reason to deny the existence of this link, but nor do I see this connection as ruling out or invalidating the kind of explanation I have put forward.

76 Ernst van de Wetering, op cit, p19.
77 Ibid, flyleaf.

78 See the discussion of these themes in Arnold Hauser, *The Social History of Art*, vol 2 (London, 1962), pp57-67.

Establishing the reasons for a certain commission or for the demand for certain kinds of works of art does not in itself explain exhaustively the nature of the artist's response to the commission or demand. Ferdinand VII's reasons for commissioning Goya to paint him clearly do not coincide with Goya's motives in carrying out the commission. In 1937 the Spanish Republican government commissioned Picasso to produce 'a work' for the Spanish pavilion in the Paris exhibition. This is not enough to 'explain' the painting of *Guernica* (though it is part of the explanation).

Also I do not find the claim that 'self-exploration' is anachronistic for Rembrandt a convincing one. A trend towards individuation and individualism is discernible in the art of the Renaissance, both in terms of the representation of individual personalities in the painting (compare Giotto with Giovanni Bellini, or Fra Angelico with Raphael or Titian), and in terms of the status and reputation of the artist with the transition from anonymous artisan to master craftsman, to 'divine' genius (Michelangelo).[78] The Reformation provides a further development of individualism in that it replaces the idea of a relationship with god mediated by the social institution of the church with the idea of a personal relationship with god through the Bible. And is it not the exploration of self in Shakespeare's *Hamlet* which has made it such an archetypal play for the bourgeois epoch? Then there is the fact that Descartes is a co-resident with Rembrandt in Amsterdam when he makes 'Cogito ergo sum' ('I think, therefore I am') the starting point of his philosophy. Bertrand Russell comments:

> *Descartes' fundamental certainty, 'I think, therefore I am', made the basis of knowledge different for each person, since for each the starting point was his own existence, not that of other individuals or of the community… Most philosophy since Descartes has had this intellectually individualistic aspect in a greater or less degree.*[79]

Finally there is the evidence of the works themselves. There are a number of works which appear to be publicity pieces or may well have been undertaken in response to market demand—for example *Rembrandt and Saskia* (c1635),[80] the *Self-Portrait Wearing a Hat* (1632), the *Self-Portrait* (1634), and the famous *Self-Portrait* (1640) in the National Gallery, where the pose is derived from Titian's *Portrait of a Man*, mentioned earlier. However, there are many others where market forces are simply not a plausible explanation for their production. There are the *tronjes* (see page 66), tiny etchings in which Rembrandt has used his own face as a model for 'heads' depicting certain emotions, such as the

79 Bertrand Russell, *History of Western Philosophy* (London, 1971), p579.

80 Also known as *'Self-Portrait' as the Prodigal Son in the Tavern*.

65

'Self-Portrait' Wide-Eyed (1640).
Rijksmuseum, Amsterdam.

'Self-Portrait' Angry (1640).
Rijksmuseum, Amsterdam.

'Self-Portrait' Open Mouthed (1640).
Rijksmuseum, Amsterdam.

1630 series of four (*'Self-Portrait' Wide-Eyed*, *'Self-Portrait' with Angry Expression*, *'Self-Portrait' Smiling* and *'Self-Portrait' Open Mouthed*). Some art historians regard these *tronjes* as purely technical exercises, practice for the depiction of emotion in history painting, but these striking little works contain a lively sharpness and a darkness which suggests an element of personal identification and self-expression. Then there are the very informal pen and ink drawings of himself at work such as *Self-Portrait Seated* (c1636) where he is shown with short tousled hair and very casual open shirt, and the beautifully simple *Full-Length Self-Portrait* (c1650) in which he stands with arms akimbo in his working clothes. Or there is the *Model Sheet with Self-Portrait* (c1651) where a single sheet shows an etching of a beggar, a self-portrait next to it, and beneath the portrait—at a 90-degree angle—a mother and child. Or the *Self-Portrait Drawing on an Etching-Plate* (c1658) in which the self-representation is so unflattering as to exclude the possibility that it was primarily market-driven.

Above all, there is the series of self-portraits from near the end of his life. From the final decade (1659-69) there are 12 full size paintings, and from the last year at least three. Just as *The Staalmeesters* is the greatest painting of its kind, so these are the finest of all self-portraits, and they immediately confront the writer with the difficulty referred to in the preface to this study—the inadequacy of anything one can write in the face of the works. Yet faced with the argument that such masterpieces are simply a response to market demand, one has to say something even if what is said is not the kind of thing that can be supported by documents or proved by evidence other than the paintings themselves. The *Self-Portrait with Beret and Turned-Up Collar* (see cover), from 1659 is an unsurpassed masterpiece of humane realism. Standing before the original in the National Gallery exhibition I felt I was seeing a living presence looming from the surface of a darkened pool. The final four self-portraits—the *Self-Portrait with Two Circles* (1665-69) which hangs in Kenwood House in north London, and the three from 1669 itself—are like a summing up of the artist's life. The Kenwood portrait shows us the old artist battered by life's woes but still standing firm and strong, monumental in his craft and his defiance. The next two, *Self-Portrait at the Age of 63* in the National Gallery and *Self-Portrait* in the Uffizi, Florence, show unmistakeable signs of decline—not decline in the artist's powers but of something starting to fail inside the man. The process seems more advanced in the Uffizi portrait than in the National Gallery one. By the time we get to what is probably the very last of the

81 William Carlos Williams, introduction to Allen Ginsberg, *Howl and Other Poems (*San Francisco, 1965), p7.

82 Arnold Hauser, op cit, pxxxii.

series, the *Self- Portrait* in the Hague Mauritshuis, the man's mainspring has gone. Yet the painting constitutes a kind of amazing paradox in that someone this broken down by life ought not to have been able to paint this picture. We enter here the territory which the American poet William Carlos Williams attempted to describe when he wrote, 'Everyone in this life is defeated, but a man, if he be a man, is not defeated'.[81]

Of course all this can be dismissed as fanciful speculation, but unless some communication of this kind is possible in art (however imperfectly or inaccurately I may have expressed it) it is hard to see any point in taking it seriously. The view that the profusion of self-portraits in Rembrandt's oeuvre is explicable in terms of consumer demand is not only false, but a reflection within art history of the ideology of the supremacy of the consumer and the omnipotence of the market. Greatly preferable is Arnold Hauser's formulation that 'it was only in a bourgeois period of art, such as the Dutch 17th century that the subjective conception of painting was possible which produced the flood of self-portraits of Rembrandt'.[82]

The anti-capitalist Rembrandt

83 Karl Marx, *The Communist Manifesto.*

84 John Berger, op cit, p112.

85 Ibid, p109.

It is a dialectical principle that any tendency pushed to its extreme turns into its opposite. So it is with bourgeois individualism—a product, indeed a great achievement, of the rise of capitalism. Individualism, taken beyond a certain point, comes into conflict with capitalist society (we should not forget Marx's description of communist society as 'an association in which the free development of each is the condition for the free development of all'[83]). This is what happens with Rembrandt's self-portraits. Analysing the 1669 Uffizi *Self-Portrait* John Berger writes:

In [this] painting he has turned the tradition against itself. He has wrested its language away from it. He is an old man. All has gone except a sense of the question of existence, of existence as a question. And the painter in him—who is both more and less than the old man—has found the means to express just that, using a medium which has been traditionally developed to exclude any such question.[84]

The tradition of oil painting to which Berger refers is a tradition obsessed with the visible representation of property, commodities and status, 'not so much a framed window open on to the world as a safe set into the wall, a safe in which the visible has been deposited'.[85] This is the tradition Rembrandt contests with weapons forged

86 Again, remember Marx in *The Communist Manifesto*: 'The weapons with which the bourgeoisie felled feudalism to the ground are now turned against the bourgeoisie itself.'

by the tradition.[86] The late self-portraits are implicitly anti-capitalist in the double sense that they are a sympathetic representation of someone who has been broken down by the vicissitudes of life in capitalist society, and that they embody an intense humanism which is incompatible with the values and norms of a society based on production for profit, not human need.

Of course the word 'implicitly' must be heavily stressed here. There can be no question of attributing to Rembrandt some kind of conscious anti-capitalist ideology or critique of capitalism. Some 150 years before Babeuf's Conspiracy of Equals in the French Revolution, 200 years before the Utopian socialists and the Chartists, never mind Marx and Engels, and with no equivalent in the Dutch Revolt of Thomas Munzer or Gerard Winstanley, Rembrandt could not possibly have held a coherent anti-capitalist political position. But he could rebel, spontaneously and intuitively, against the experience of capitalist social relations, against the way capitalism treated people and, unlike most such spontaneous and intuitive rebels, he had a means of expressing his rebellion in his work.

In fact rebellious, critical and implicitly anti-capitalist elements are not at all confined to Rembrandt's last works or even to the period of his own financial difficulties and relative lack of success after 1656. On the contrary, they are present throughout his career, including during the period of his early success, even if only in latent form and even if they remain subordinate to the dominant bourgeois elements. Their most basic manifestation is in what Rembrandt does not paint. Of the various genres of Dutch art it is noticeable that Rembrandt produces almost no still lifes—he has no interest in *trompe l'oeil* effects or the naturalistic rendering of food and other commodities for its own sake—and no paintings of sea battles or marine paintings of any kind and, virtually nothing that was in any way militaristic, except the special case of *The Night Watch* (see page 22), which will be discussed shortly. Either Rembrandt had no interest in matters naval, colonial and martial, or he received no such commissions because the authorities in these areas had no interest in his style of painting, or both.

In sharp contrast there is his remarkable predilection for depicting the outcasts and outsiders of Dutch society. In his career as a whole Rembrandt etched or drew more than 25 images of beggars and several others of poor people whose situation was not far removed from beggary, such as the etchings of *The Rat Killer* (1632), *The Spanish Gypsy* (1642) and *Peasant Family on the Tramp* (1652). Of these, 16 or 17 were done before he reached

87 'Prints of beggars by the French artist Callot were popular in Holland at this time... But what a difference! Callot's beggars are picturesque: at best sentimental, at worst designed to please those who derive pleasure from looking at those less fortunate than themselves.' Charles Fowkes, op cit, p39. See also John Berger's comments on Dutch genre painting in *Ways of Seeing*, op cit, p103-104, and my discussion of Richard Billingham's photographs of his family in John Molyneux, 'State of the Art', *International Socialism* 79 (Summer 1998) pp101-102.

88 Kenneth Clark, *An Introduction to Rembrandt* (London, 1978), p43.

89 Cited ibid.

the age of 25 in 1631, and it seems reasonable to suppose that many of them were drawn from life in Leiden, where pauperism was particularly intense. I have already described the treatment of, and prevailing attitude towards, beggars in the Dutch republic. In such a context Rembrandt's studies are an act of defiance. Here we encounter the leper with his clapper, the beggar with a wooden leg (see page 54), the seated beggar warming his hands, the seated beggar with his dog, the blind fiddler led by his dog on a string, the gaunt mother begging with a child in her arms (the contemporary resonance is unmistakeable). Of course, it is not the subject matter itself but its treatment that determines the nature of the work. It has always been possible to picture the poor sentimentally or voyeuristically or as curiosities, but there is no trace of these attitudes here.[87] Kenneth Clark refers to Rembrandt's 'sympathy for poor people',[88] and provides documentary support in the form of testimony from a contemporary, Joachim von Sandrart, who complained that Rembrandt 'did not at all know how to keep his station, and always associated with the lower orders'.[89] But sympathy is not quite the right word for the standpoint of these works. Identification and solidarity are nearer the mark, as evidenced by what is perhaps the most extraordinary of all this series, namely the etching *Beggar Seated on a Bank* (1630), where he portrays himself as a beggar (see page 54).

90 See Jonathan Israel, op cit, pp376-377, and A T van Deursen, op cit, pp32-33.

Another marginal group who were frequently the focus of Rembrandt's attention were the Jews. The Amsterdam Jews benefited from the unique religious tolerance operating in Dutch society—that is why they came there from Spain and Central Europe—but they remained outsiders nonetheless, and were subject to a degree of oppression.[90] It is sometimes said that Rembrandt was attracted to the Jews as subjects because he saw in them the people of the Old Testament. Be that as it may, personal association and friendship also played a major part as Rembrandt's house in Amsterdam, until forced by poverty to move in 1658, was located in Sint-Anthonisbreistraat (today Judenbreestraat—the Jewish Broad Street) in the heart of the Jewish quarter. The Jewish community was divided into Sephardim from Spain known as 'marranos' (swine) who fled the Inquisition, and Ashkenazim from Germany who fled the Thirty Years War. The Sephardim were few in number but tended to be wealthy and educated. The Ashkenazim were more numerous but poorer and less cultured. Rembrandt painted and etched them both. Of the Sephardim, who were freer in their attitude to graven images, we get named and commissioned portraits such

91 Charles Fowkes, op cit, p91.
92 K G Boon, *Rembrandt: The Complete Etchings* (London, 1963), pii.
93 For example there are four anonymous *Old Man* paintings from 1629 alone (when Rembrandt was 22 to 23).

74

as *The Jewish Physician Ephraim Bueno* (1647) and the etching of the famous rabbi *Manasseh ben Israel*. Of the Ashkenazim we get studies of anonymous figures such as the *Portrait of a Young Jew* (1661) and the highly unusual etching of *The Synagogue* (1648). Then there is the equally unusual series of portraits of Christ with Jewish features (I count nine). All in all, Fowkes calculates that 'of 200 male portraits…which the artist made, 37, nearly one fifth, are identified as Jews: a remarkably high number since Jews represented little more than 1 percent of the city's population'.[91]

To this we can add Rembrandt's portrayal of blacks—there are about six works in all, including a wonderful double portrait, *Two Negroes* (1661) (see page 22), which contains not a hint of racial stereotyping—and his interest in people, art and things Asian. Not only do we have three paintings of men in oriental costume, all strongly sympathetic, but also a number of copies of miniatures from Moghul India including, fascinatingly, a drawing of Shah Jehan (who 'built' the Taj Mahal). Regarding the Indian miniatures K G Boon comments, 'He was probably the first European to recognise their unique beauty'.[92] Finally there is Rembrandt's deeply affectionate representation of old people, which begins in his early twenties,[93] and his uniquely anti-sexist portrayal of women, discussed earlier.

Running through Rembrandt's depictions of the oppressed is one of the most distinctive characteristics of his art—the ability to paint or draw from 'inside' the mind and body of his subjects. As John Berger has said, this is contrary to the dominant tradition of European oil painting which is one of exteriorisation. Normally the artist paints with the eye of the observer—the voyeur or perhaps lover in most nudes, the prostitute's client (in Manet's *Olympia* and Picasso's *Demoiselles D'Avignon*), the visitor to the house in a de Hooch interior, to the estate in Gainsborough's *Mr and Mrs Andrews*. The reversal of this relationship is a 'political' characteristic—it is 'solidarity in paint'. It is not present in all Rembrandt's works, in many of the society portraits, even in the masterpieces like *The Anatomy Lesson* and *The Staalmeesters,* or his paintings of Saskia as Flora, for instance, but it is a key factor in some of the 'oddities' we find scattered through his oeuvre, moments of disturbance which often upset or puzzle the art historians because they are so 'different'.

I shall give four examples. First *The Rape of Proserpine* (c1628-29). The abduction of Proserpine by Pluto, king of the underworld, was a well known classical theme from Ovid also treated by Rubens and others. In Rubens Proserpine is shown with her arms dramatically

94 Kenneth Clark, *Rembrandt and the Italian Renaissance*, op cit, p10.

flung back over her head. In Rembrandt she is clawing at Pluto's face. Kenneth Clark comments:

> *[Rembrandt's] sense of truth would not allow him to accept the ineffectual eloquence of those flung-back arms, with which, by classical convention, Sabine women and other heroines of antique legend convey the information that they are being raped. What in fact would a decent young Dutch girl do in the situation? Kick and scratch: scratch his eyes out.*[94]

Clark notices the key difference but misunderstands and makes light of it. It is not about down to earth Dutch realism—it is about identification. Rembrandt is 'with' Proserpine—Rubens and Clark are not.

Second, *The Rape of Ganymede* (1635). Once again the story comes from Ovid who tells how Jove 'burned with love' for the young Ganymede and transformed himself into an eagle to whisk him off to be his servant and plaything in Olympus. Rembrandt's dark and dramatic painting is clearly derived, but also different, from an engraving by Barbizet which is taken from a lost original by Michelangelo. In the Barbizet/Michelangelo version Ganymede is a beautiful young man who submits ecstatically to the grip of the great bird-god. In Rembrandt Ganymede is a young child, almost a baby, who screams and urinates in terror at his sudden seizure. The contrast has occasioned much debate, with the Rembrandt being called, absurdly, 'a comedy' and 'a grotesque parody', and by Kenneth Clark 'a protest not only against antique art, but against antique morality', and 'a protestant-Christian revulsion against the sexual practices of paganism that Michelangelo's version so clearly implies'.[95] Whatever the truth of this, one factor in Rembrandt's treatment is simply that Rembrandt is feeling 'with' Ganymede.

My third example is one of Rembrandt's most extraordinary works, *The Slaughtered Ox* (1655) (see page 22).[96] It is extraordinary in the sense that it fits none of the standard genres of the time (though, of course, the subject reaches back to the caves of Lascaux and forward to Damien Hirst) except, formally, still life. In fact it is anything but a still life—nothing could be further removed from an edible lobster. Rembrandt's ox is flayed, splayed and crucified upside down, like St Peter, on a frame. Hélène Cixous writes almost poetically:

Why do we adore The Slaughtered Ox? *Because without our knowing it or wanting it, it is our anonymous humanity...*

We are this creature, which even turned upside down and decapitated and hung beneath the earth—when it is seen with those eyes that don't reject the below, that don't prefer the above—maintains its majesty.

Behold the portrait of our mortality. The being hung

95 Ibid, pp12–13. A significant participant in this debate and in the general debate on Rembrandt is Nicos Hadjinicolaou, *Art History and Class Struggle* (London, 1978), who mocks Clark's reaction and cites *The Rape of Ganymede* as an example of 'critical baroque visual ideology' (pp163-68). Hadjinicolaou attempts a rather mechanical application of Althusserian structuralist 'Marxism' to the discipline of art history. It is tempting to discuss the strengths and weaknesses of his approach and judgements at some length (it would require quite a long discussion) but time and space do not permit this. However, I disagree strongly with his tendency to reduce art to ideology.

96 There are two versions of *The Slaughtered Ox*, one from 1635 and one from 1655. The experts say that the earlier work is probably not by Rembrandt himself. Both are fine paintings but the later work, which I refer to here, is much more powerful.

97 Hélène Cixous, 'Bathsheba or the Interior Bible' in *Stigmata: Escaping Texts* (London, 1998), pp15-16.

(by its shins), turned upside down, twice decapitated.

What we become under the axe and the slicer. There is a butcher shop on our life's path. As children we would pass trembling before the butcher's window. Later on we want to forget death. We cut the dead one up into pieces and we call it meat.[97]

The poetics are justified because Rembrandt has painted from within the ox.

Finally there is a small drawing of *A Woman on the Gallows* (1664). This is Rembrandt's judgement on the Dutch republic's justice system. Apparently drawn from life, it depicts a Danish girl hanging in chains on the gibbet, with an axe, the instrument of her crime, displayed beside her. It is the simplest of drawings and yet it exudes the profoundest sympathy with this poor little woman, her eyes closed in death, her narrow shoulders hunched against the rope and her tiny arms hanging limply before her. The death penalty always poses directly the question—whose side are you on? Not between the victim of crime and the criminal as the right would have it, but between the state and its victim. Here Rembrandt gives his quiet but definitive answer. He draws from 'inside' the woman on the gallows.

How is all this anti-capitalist? It is simply that this degree of human solidarity cannot fail to clash with the logic and priorities of a system driven by the competitive accumulation of capital. Capitalism rests on alienated labour.[98] The alienation of labour results in the alienation of workers not only from the products of their labour, but from themselves, from their fellows and from nature. Rembrandt's art, his creative labour, is continually trying to challenge these alienations, to reach out across these divisions.

Any argument about the anti-capitalist implications of Rembrandt's art must deal with the question of what is possibly his most famous painting, though by no means his best, *The Night Watch*, or *The Militia Company of Captain Frans Banning Cocq* (1642) (see page 22), even though this is something of a diversion. This is because for a long time a myth surrounded this painting—a myth which informed by far the best known account of his life, namely Alexander Korda's 1937 film with Charles Laughton in the title role. *The Night Watch* was an example of the common genre of Dutch painting known as 'schutterij', paintings of companies of civic guards who had played an important role defending Dutch cities in the revolt against Spain, and who had also taken on a certain law and order policing role. The story was that members of the company paid Rembrandt 100 guilders each for the commission, but were bitterly disappointed

98 See Marx's analysis of alienated labour in his *Economic and Philosophic Manuscripts*. Karl Marx, *Early Writings* (London, 1963), pp120-134.

99 Simon Schama has made a detailed analysis of this dynamic composition in *Rembrandt's Eyes*, op cit, pp496-500.

by the result because of the painting's darkness and failure to provide a satisfactory portrait of each guard, and that this was the start of the artist's descent into isolation and poverty. Art historians today are virtually unanimous that there is no evidence to support this tale, and that there is plenty of evidence to show that Rembrandt continued to receive prestigious commissions.

However, it is not difficult to see how the legend arose for, circumstantial and documentary evidence aside, the painting itself provides evidence that it was a radical and challenging work. The Amsterdam Rijksmuseum displays *The Night Watch* alongside other paintings of militia companies by contemporaries such as Bartholomeus van der Helst, Joachim von Sandrart and Thomas de Keyser. The difference is striking. In the latter paintings the companies are lined up and arranged in a static pose, rather like a wedding photograph, with each guard's head clearly depicted and more or less equally lit (as are the surgeons in Rembrandt's *Anatomy Lesson of Dr Nicolaes Tulp*). In *The Night Watch* the company is presented in apparently chaotic, but in fact carefully structured, dynamic movement marching out of the darkness into the light.[99] Some figures (a rather inappropriate but brightly lit girl and a shadowy dog) have been added. Others are pushed into the background or half hidden by outstretched arms. It is clear that what Rembrandt has done is subordinate the requirements of the commission to his own purposes as an artist, to his own urge to create a complex symphony of movement and light. As his pupil, Samuel van Hoogstraten, put it in 1678: '…in the opinion of many he went too far, making more of the overall picture according to his individual preference than of the individual portraits he was commissioned to do'.[100]

100 Cited ibid, p488.

If Rembrandt got away with *The Night Watch* he was less fortunate with what was probably the biggest commission he ever received, the order in 1660 from the Amsterdam city fathers to paint *The Conspiracy of the Batavians* (*The Conspiracy of Claudius Civilis: The Oath*) for the new town hall. The commission was for a vast painting of great patriotic significance because the Dutch bourgeoisie viewed the rebellion of Claudius Civilis against the Romans as the forerunner of their own revolt against the Spanish, much as the English view Queen Boudicca or Alfred the Great. Unfortunately Rembrandt's painting remained in the town hall for only a few months before it was rejected as unsatisfactory. As a result Rembrandt, desperate for money by this time, cut the huge painting down to make it saleable, and only the truncated fragment remains. Documentary evidence of the reasons for

101 Kenneth Clark, who refers repeatedly to Rembrandt the rebel in both his books on the artist, is unable to answer this question seriously and reduces Rembrandt's artistic radicalism to (a) a personal character trait and (b) a rebellion against Italian classicism.

102 Artistically speaking. Politically William Morris was a revolutionary socialist and identified with the working class.

103 In Pound's case his critique of capitalism and idealisation of medieval Provence, the troubadours, Dante, etc, led him straight into the arms of Mussolini.

the rejection has not survived (which means there is much speculative debate), but clearly Rembrandt's mystic eerie treatment, reminiscent in my opinion of the atmosphere in *Macbeth* and *King Lear*, was deemed inappropriate for the purpose of the invention of heroic nationalist tradition.

Rembrandt's artistic solidarity with the oppressed in Dutch society and the clash at certain points between his art and the requirements of the Dutch bourgeoisie raises the question of what values he counterposed to rampant Dutch capitalism. In the name of what did he rebel?[101] As we have said, it was not and could not have been in the name of a worked out socialist programme or a revolutionary proletariat, or even a revolutionary peasantry (there was no significant peasant revolt in the United Provinces). It might possibly have been in the name of a former 'golden age' set far in the past à la Rousseau, or an idealised feudalism like the pre-Raphaelites or William Morris[102] or Ezra Pound,[103] or a romanticised nature as in Wordsworth, Keats and even Shelley at times. But it was not any of these things. Nor do such tendencies appear to have existed to any degree in Dutch society. Rather Rembrandt's rebellion seems to have been in the name of a profound personal humanitarianism, a deep personal tenderness and intimacy—'the intimacy of intimacy, intimitude'[104] as Cixous calls it—one might say 'love' if the word had not been so trivialised and exploited.

This seems to fit with, or at least to be compatible with, the known facts of Rembrandt's life: with his gradual withdrawal from the social scene from the late 1640s onwards, following the death of Saskia and a dreadful relationship with Geertje Dircx,[105] into the bosom of his new 'family' with Hendrickje and Titus; with his and Hendrickje's conflict with the church authorities over their 'living in sin' (in 1654 Hendrickje was summoned four times to appear before the council of the Reformed Church—three times she did not go but on the fourth she did and was condemned for practising 'whoredom'); and with the intensification of his retreat after his bankruptcy in 1656. It also fits, again and again, with the work. Two of his last works, which exemplify the quality I am talking about, are *The Return of the Prodigal Son* (c1668) (see page 54), and *The Jewish Bride* (c1668) (see page 8).

The Return of the Prodigal Son depicts the denouement of the parable when the lost son is forgiven by his father. As Arnold Hauser has noticed, the painting dematerialises reality in a way reminiscent of Michelangelo's last work, the *Rondanini Pietà*.[106] The

104 Hélène Cixous, op cit, p7. This project has been five years in the making, and the overall argument and conclusion has been present almost since the beginning, but it was only right at the end that I came across this Cixous neologism that so well expresses my meaning.
105 This ended with Rembrandt scheming to have Geertje condemned to a house of correction, where she remained for five years—an act of cruelty for which it is hard to imagine any justification, although, or course, we do not know anything like the full story.
106 See Arnold Hauser, op cit, pxxxiii, pxix and pp106-107.

four standing figures are ungrounded. They float spectre like in the darkness. The head of the son is barely more than a modelled outline, his body almost wasted beneath his rough clothes. The only really substantial part of the painting, the only thing that really counts, is the father's gesture of reconciliation, the diamond of his arms embracing the head and shoulders of the boy. It is the placing of the hands that is decisive, not clutching, grabbing or seizing, but open and flat, fingers slightly apart resting lightly but firmly on the shoulder and upper back, the essence of compassion and reassurance.

The Prodigal Son reminds us how often hands and the gestures of hands play a central role in Rembrandt's paintings. At the beginning of this study I noted the absence of hands in *The Rokeby Venus* (see page 12), and elsewhere in the representation of nude women, and pointed to the contrast in Rembrandt's *Bathsheba*. Then there is the dark silhouetted hand at the centre of *The Apostle Peter Denying Christ* (1660); the hand of the dying old man caressing the head of the child in *Jacob Blessing the Children of Joseph* (1656); the hands of the surgeon at the head of the corpse in *The Anatomy Lesson of Doctor Deyman* (1656); the hand of the philosopher reaching out to the poet in *Aristotle Contemplating a Bust of Homer* (1653); the astonishing right hand of Abraham clasping the face of Isaac, at once violent and gentle, and the hand of the angel gripping Abraham's left wrist before he can strike at his son's throat in *The Angel Stopping Abraham from Sacrificing Isaac to God* (1635); the upturned outstretched right hand of Captain Cocq at the focal point of *The Night Watch*; the gesture of wonder and welcome in *The Danaë*; the arm of the woman criss-crossing with the arm of the cherub and her fingers resting on his cheek in *Hendrickje Stoffels as Venus* (1658); and many others. It is not a trick or trademark—there are many more works in which hands do not appear or are not particularly important—but it is a motif to which Rembrandt returns, consciously or unconsciously, again and again: the helping hand, the hand of friendship, the touch of love, the hand that is the mark of our humanity.

Now let us turn to *The Jewish Bride*.[107] It is a sublime masterpiece in which 40 years of accumulated craft and experience in the laying of paint on canvas are brought to bear, not for a display of virtuosity but in order to make a visual statement about the potential for love between two human beings. The atmosphere of the painting derives in considerable part from the clothes of the couple. The technique deployed here is the equal of Holbein's in *The Ambassadors* or Bellini's in *The Doge*, but it does its best to conceal itself, and the clothes have

107 The title is from the 19th century and it is not known who the couple were or if they were really Jewish, but this is of little significance.

85

108 Karl Marx, *The Communist Manifesto*, op cit.

nothing to do with marking the status of the sitters. They are there for colour. The coral red of the bride's dress combines with the dark and shining golds of the groom's tunic and cloak to create a mellow warmth that suffuses the canvas. Within this glow it is the positioning of the hands that holds the eye and delivers the painting's emotional message. His left hand resting lightly on her left shoulder and drawing her in; his right hand crossing her right arm and alighting open-palmed on her breast in the gentlest of caresses; her left hand just grazing his knuckles in acceptance. A tenderness unsurpassed in European art and not without reason, for it is the antithesis of capitalist competition and exploitation, bourgeois marriage as prostitution, alienation and reification, and the reduction of human beings to 'appendages of the machine'.[108]

Rembrandt, tragedy and history

Rembrandt's dates were 1606-69. The following great artists were his contemporaries, slightly older or slightly younger: Pieter Paul Rubens 1577-1640, Frans Hals 1581-1666, Nicolas Poussin 1593-1665, Anthony Van Dyck 1599-1641, Diego Velázquez 1599-1660, Claude Lorraine 1600-82, Jacob Van Ruisdael 1628-82, and Jan Vermeer 1632-75.

This is a rich crop. Depending on one's judgement it includes at least three of the supreme masters in the history of oil painting. There is a very clear stylistic division between the Dutch (Hals, Ruisdael and Vermeer), the artists of the revolutionary bourgeois republic, and the rest who, whether classical or baroque, Flemish, French or Spanish, remained on the ground of the old order. But there is also an immediately obvious difference between Rembrandt and all the others. In Rembrandt's work, viewed as a whole, there is a deep sadness, a quite distinctive tragic vision. I do not mean by this that all or even a numerical majority of his works are overtly sad or tragic. That is clearly not true of most of the society portraits, for example, but it is true of most of the best pictures, especially the later ones where there is an underlying sadness even in those paintings such as *The*

109 Christopher White, *Rembrandt* (London, 1984), p206.
110 Charles Fowkes, op cit, p12.
111 See Trotsky's discussion of this question in 'Class and Art', in *Leon Trotsky On Literature and Art* (New York, 1977), pp63-82.

Staalmeesters that are ostensibly celebratory and positive.

What is the basis of this tragic vision? The standard response of art historians is to refer here to Rembrandt's 'universality', his transcendence of historically limited conditions through his tackling of 'universal' themes such as love and death, and his expression of 'timeless' emotions. Thus Christopher White tells us that Rembrandt's works, 'although created at one time in one place...possess a timeless universal validity',[109] and Charles Fowkes writes that 'Rembrandt, like Shakespeare...uses his art to convey ideas which apply to human beings of all times and all cultures'.[110]

Such claims raise complex issues which cannot be properly debated here, but these formulations are unsatisfactory. Yes, there are certain permanent features of the human condition, death being the most obvious and indisputable one, and, even more importantly, profound continuities across long periods of history, such as the existence of rich and poor, or the oppression of women. Moreover these continuities make possible the ongoing appeal and emotive power of certain works of art over long periods of time and in different historical epochs.[111] But lasting 'a long time', even centuries or millennia, does not amount to 'forever' or 'all time' or the transcendence of history. The English monarchy has a long history—it is not 'universal' or 'timeless'. Death is universal and class divisions have existed for 5,000 years or more, but people respond differently to death and class in different situations and different cultures. Also, a distinction must be made between production and reception. Art, as Trotsky used to say, is 'a function of the nerves',[112] so the immediacy and urgency of an idea or emotion have to be far more intense for it to generate a work of art than for that art to be appreciated or enjoyed. No one today can write like Chaucer or paint like Breughel, but their work can still offer us something.[113] Even so, depending on the degree of social change and continuity and the nature of the art, work that was once a living part of culture can fade to the point where it is only of interest to academic specialists. Rembrandt, emphatically, has not so much faded, but that does not make his work in general or his tragic vision in particular into something 'timeless' or outside history. On the contrary, as it has been the whole purpose of this study to argue, Rembrandt's work was a response to a very specific historical situation, but not to the superficial features of that situation, to its deepest social and historical forces, its most fundamental contradictions, and it is this which explains the sense of tragedy emanating from so many of his paintings.

Like others at the time Rembrandt experienced

112 Ibid, p106.

113 Karl Marx makes this same point in relation to ancient Greek art in his 'Introduction' to Karl Marx, *The Grundrisse,* (London, 1973), pp110-111, though I do not find Marx's explanation of Greek art's survival very convincing.

89

the birth of bourgeois society as an immense step forward for himself and his people, as not only economic and political progress but as a great liberation for the human personality, and he had good reason for doing so. However, he also lived long enough with this capitalist society to observe and experience in his own life its negative sides, its exploitation and alienation, its colonialism and its cruelty, its profiteering and its ruthlessness. But the humanitarian values he clung to in the face of this society were impotent before the remorseless march of capital. In the absence of a social force able to challenge capitalism and embody an alternative to it two centuries before the emergence of the modern working class, this humanitarianism was destined only to be crushed and defeated, forced back into the realm of the most private and intimate. Yet in his work he did not abandon it—he celebrated it, defended it and mourned its fate. He chose this defeat over any of the possible victories on offer.

To make this analysis more concrete let us look at my final exhibit (see page 7), *The Man with the Golden Helmet.*

This was painted somewhere between 1648 and 1650, that is at the time of, or just after, the Treaty of Munster in 1648 which brought the Eighty Years War to an end and set the seal on the independent existence of the Dutch republic. It presents us with an old man, an old soldier. It has been said that the face resembles Rembrandt's brother Adrien, and that perhaps Adrien was the model, but this is irrelevant. The helmet makes the old man a soldier, a battle-hardened veteran, his face lined with care, his brow furrowed in thought. The eyes half look at us and are half blank. Behind them the soldier is lost in contemplation. This man has seen the blood and the pity of war. The wondrously painted helmet turns all symbolism inside out. A helmet is a military symbol, but not this helmet. This is not a military painting. Gold is a symbol of wealth and power. A golden helmet signifies wealth, power and military glory—a golden helmet for the golden age. But not this helmet. Even though it is 'real' gold, though you can feel its weight and lustre, not an ounce of swagger or triumph attaches to this helmet. Plumes signify pomp and circumstance, pride and vanity, but not these plumes. The helmet and the face complement one another but also criticise each other. Every brushstroke criticises the world that made this old man what he is, but it is a resigned, tragic critique, a critique without hope, except for the hope that the painting itself represents by virtue of its being created, and the hope that we in different times, far worse and far better, can wrest from it.

There is an irony lurking here, a twist in the tail. According to the experts of the Rembrandt Research Project in Amsterdam, who have been busy for years reassessing and reattributing the works hitherto assigned to Rembrandt, *The Man with the Golden Helmet* is not, or is probably not, by Rembrandt at all, but by a member of his workshop called Willem Drost. Such assessments are, of course, made on the basis of much 'scientific' research (X-rays and such) and immense technical knowledge, but the obsession with provenance and attribution is driven by two considerations: first, the traditional bourgeois idea of genius which makes the work simply an effect, an epiphenomenon, of the artist's inborn or god-given talent; and second, the question of paintings' market value which, because of the aforesaid idea of genius, depends more on the fame of the presumed painter than on the artistic merit of the work. The two come together in the form of collectors and dealers who will pay $60 million for an 'authentic' Rembrandt, but only a few hundred thousand dollars for the same painting if it is 'proved' to be by someone other than 'the master', and galleries and museums which will fight tooth and nail to defend the 'authenticity' of their collections and the value of their investments.

But *The Man with the Golden Helmet* turns the

tables on this bourgeois individualist view of art and art history. If in mid-17th century Amsterdam there was more than one person capable of painting this picture, not only the legendary Rembrandt but also the relatively unknown Willem Drost, then what stronger proof could one find of the role of social conditions and historical circumstances in shaping the production of art? The great Marxist historian Christopher Hill in an old book review in the *New Statesman*, summed the matter up as follows:

The United Netherlands in the 17th century is one of the miracles of world history. A tiny people of 2 million, disunited in religion and by intense provincial loyalties, won independence from the mighty empire of Spain. Within a generation it became a leading naval and colonial power which also set the pace for Europe in arts and sciences, with Grotius, Rembrandt, Huygens and Spinoza... [This] book presents us with all the paradox of a high civilisation built on exploitation, greed and hypocrisy.[114]

The argument of this booklet is that 'one of the miracles of world history' was met and matched by one of the miracles of world art.

114 Christopher Hill in the *New Statesman*, cited on the cover of C R Boxer, *The Dutch Seaborne Empire: 1600-1800* (London, 1977).

For other publications from Redwords go to:
www.redwords.org.uk